Playing Piano with Thr

Folk Songs

Arranged by Robert Schultz

MW00575176

CONTENTS

Playing Piano with Three Chords

Playing Piano with Three Chords is a series written for the late-elementary pianist. It is an introduction to basic chord playing, harmonizing, and hands-together playing.

The contents have been carefully selected to appeal to late-elementary pianists of all ages, and to provide familiar melodies that are well suited to basic harmonization with easy, chord-based accompaniments. Melodies are harmonized with no more than three chords, usually the primary triads (I, IV, V or V7) in easy key signatures.

A diagram of the basic chord progression used in each arrangement is provided at the beginning of the arrangement. In this diagram the chords are presented in block form for preliminary practice—first in root position, then in the inversions used in the arrangement. Chord names are included in each diagram as well as within the arrangement. In addition to block chords, students will be introduced to simple broken-chord accompaniments in several of the arrangements.

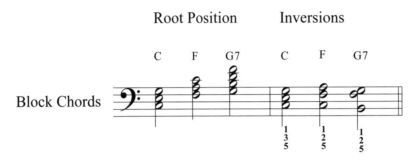

Pieces appear in order of difficulty. The editing is appropriate for the late-elementary pianist, including fundamental dynamics, articulations, phrase marks, and necessary fingering. Every effort has been made to provide high quality, educationally sound arrangements that serve as stepping stones to higher levels while satisfying the student's desire to play popular and familiar music.

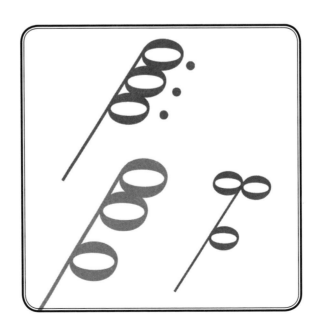

Merrily We Roll Along

Traditional American
arr. Robert Schultz

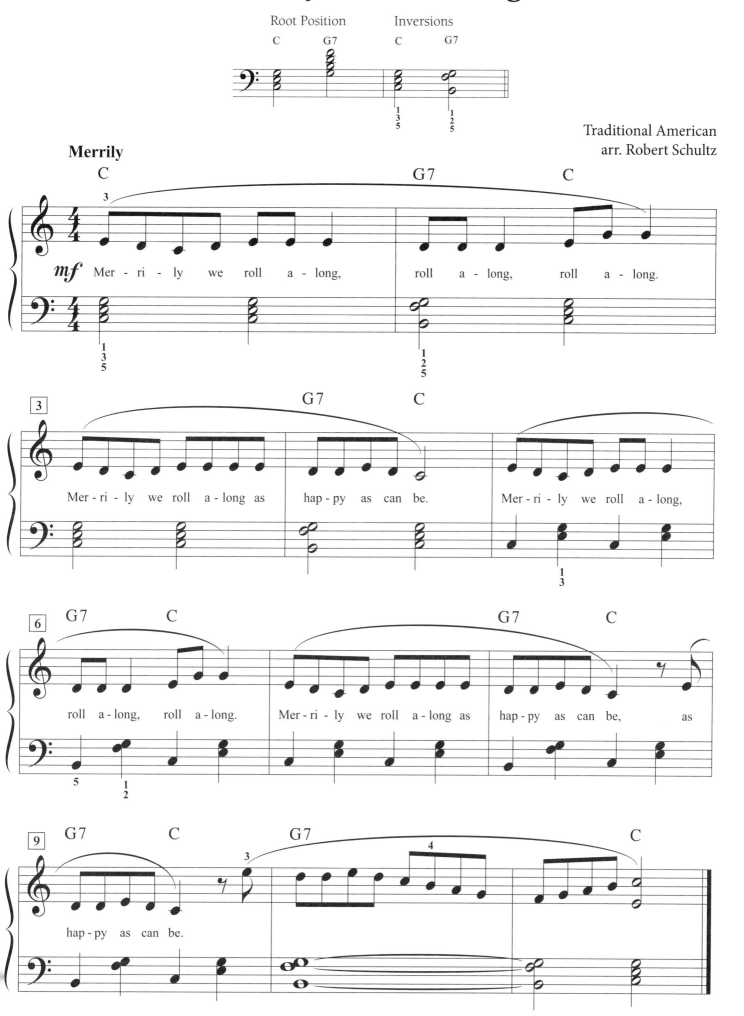

Camptown Races

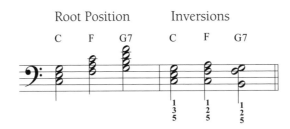

Stephen Foster
arr. Robert Schultz

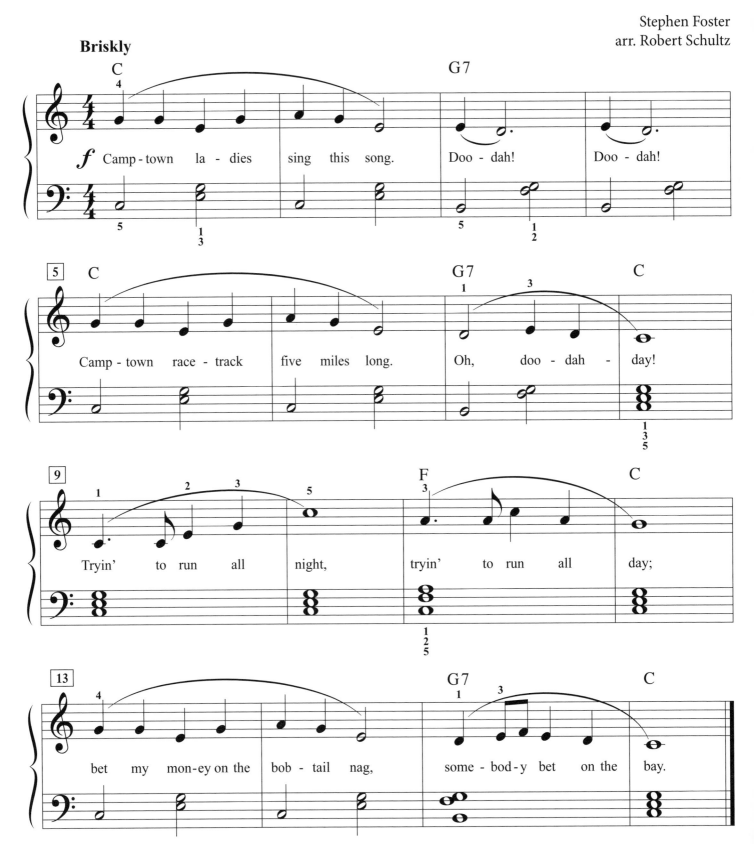

Oh! Susanna

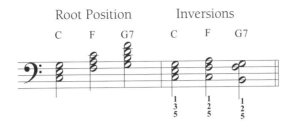

Stephen Foster
arr. Robert Schultz

She'll Be Comin' Round the Mountain

Traditional American
arr. Robert Schultz

The Yellow Rose of Texas

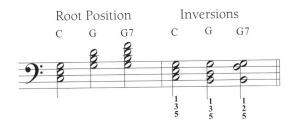

Traditional American
arr. Robert Schultz

With spirit

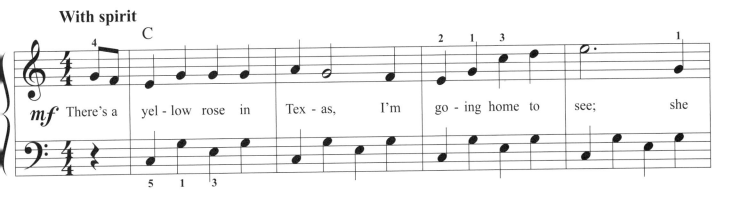

There's a yel - low rose in Tex - as, I'm go - ing home to see; she

wants no oth - er fel - low, no - bod - y, on - ly me. Oh, she

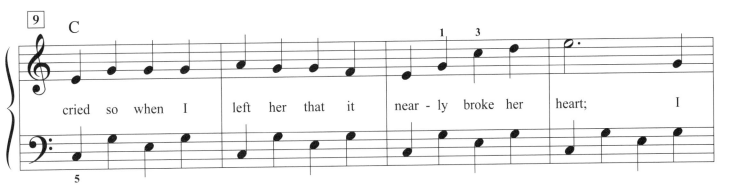

cried so when I left her that it near - ly broke her heart; I

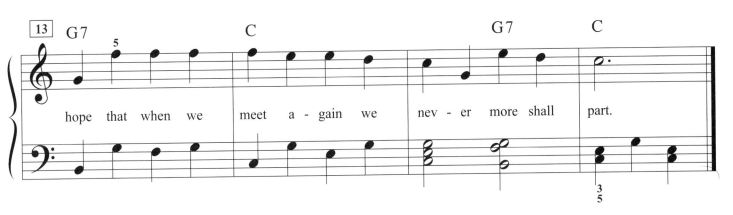

hope that when we meet a - gain we nev - er more shall part.

FJH2305

Polly Wolly Doodle

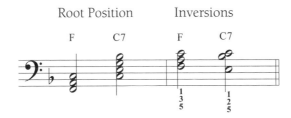

Traditional American
arr. Robert Schultz

fay,   for I'm   goin' to Lou-'si-an-a   for to   see my Su-sie-an-na, sing

Pol - ly   Wol - ly   Doo - dle   all   the   day.

Down in the Valley

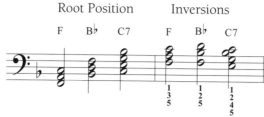

Traditional Irish
arr. Robert Schultz

Sometimes I Feel Like a Motherless Child

African-American Spiritual
arr. Robert Schultz

Hey Diddle Diddle

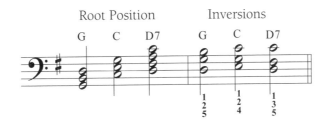

Traditional English
arr. Robert Schultz

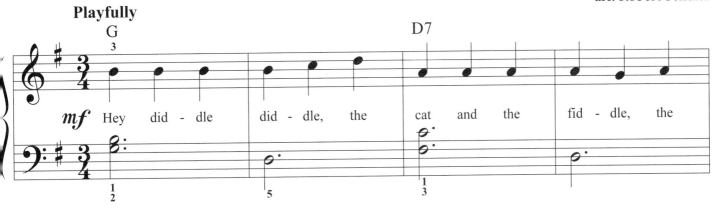

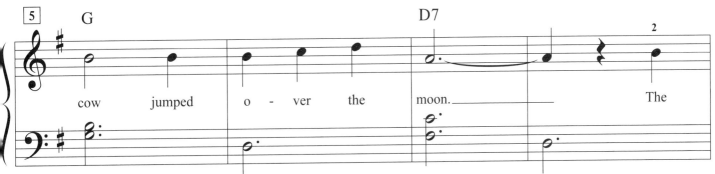

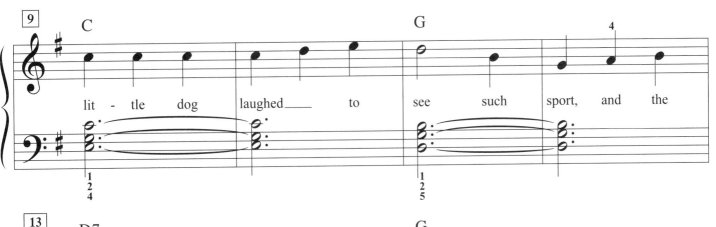

The Streets of Laredo

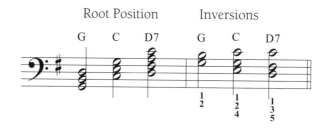

Traditional American
arr. Robert Schultz

All the Pretty Little Horses

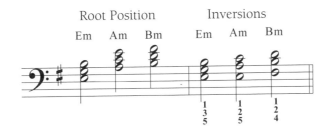

Traditional American
arr. Robert Schultz

Moderately

Hush - a - bye, don't you cry, go to sleep my lit - tle ba - by.

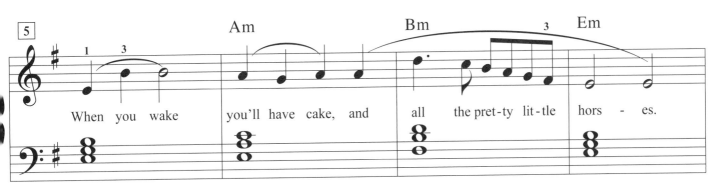

When you wake you'll have cake, and all the pret - ty lit - tle hors - es.

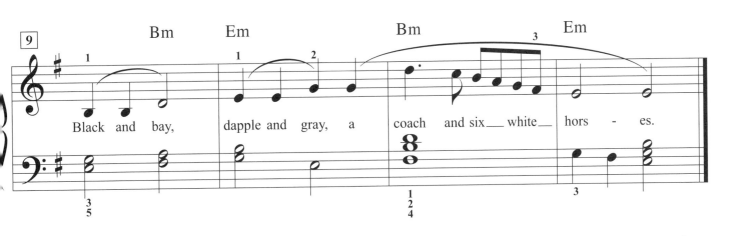

Black and bay, dapple and gray, a coach and six ___ white ___ hors - es.

FJH2305

Clementine

Traditional American
arr. Robert Schultz

Yankee Doodle

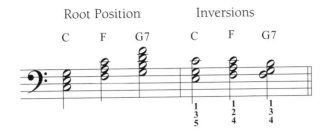

Traditional Anglo-American
arr. Robert Schultz

March tempo

Yan - kee Doo - dle went to town, rid - ing on a po - ny;

stuck a feath - er in his cap and called it mac - a - ro - ni!

Yan - kee Doo - dle keep it up, Yan - kee Doo - dle dan - dy;

mind the mu - sic and the step, and with the girls be hand - y.

My Bonnie Lies Over the Ocean

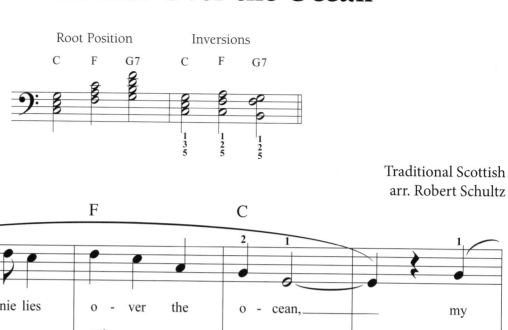

Traditional Scottish
arr. Robert Schultz

Hush, Little Baby

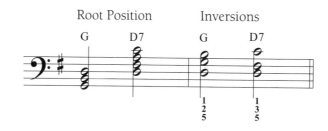

Traditional American
arr. Robert Schultz

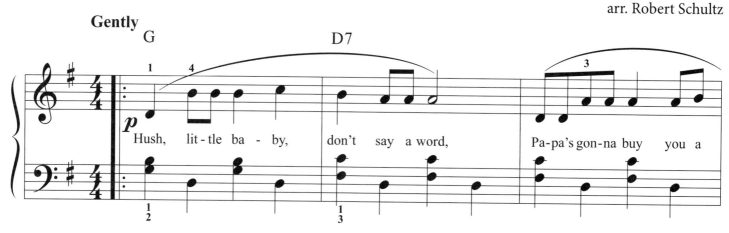

Gently

Hush, lit - tle ba - by, don't say a word, Pa - pa's gon - na buy you a

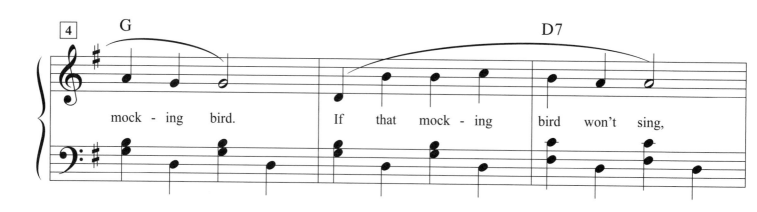

mock - ing bird. If that mock - ing bird won't sing,

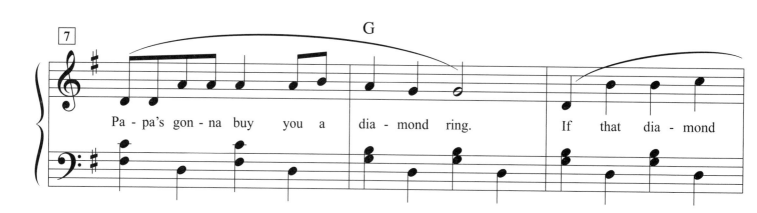

Pa - pa's gon - na buy you a dia - mond ring. If that dia - mond

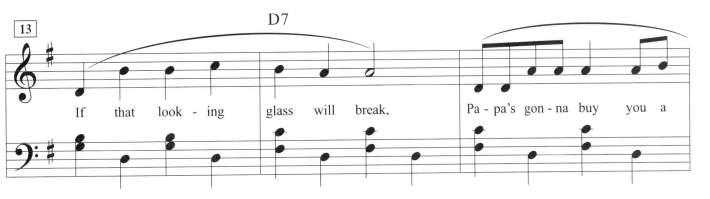

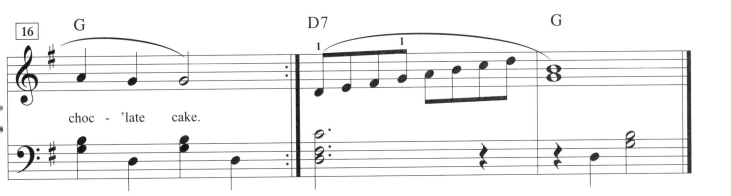

When the chocolate cake you eat,
Papa's gonna buy you a puppy sweet.
If that puppy will not bark,
Papa's gonna buy you a horse and cart.

If that horse and cart break down,
Papa's gonna buy you a big toy clown.
Hush, little baby, don't you cry,
Mama's gonna sing you a lullaby.

Auld Lang Syne

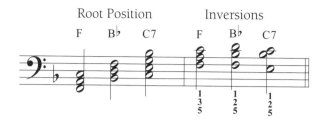

Traditional Scottish
arr. Robert Schultz

Did You Ever See a Lassie?

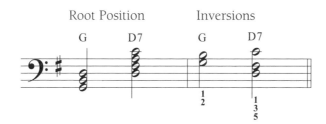

Traditional Scottish-American
arr. Robert Schultz

The Bear Went Over the Mountain

Traditional
arr. Robert Schultz

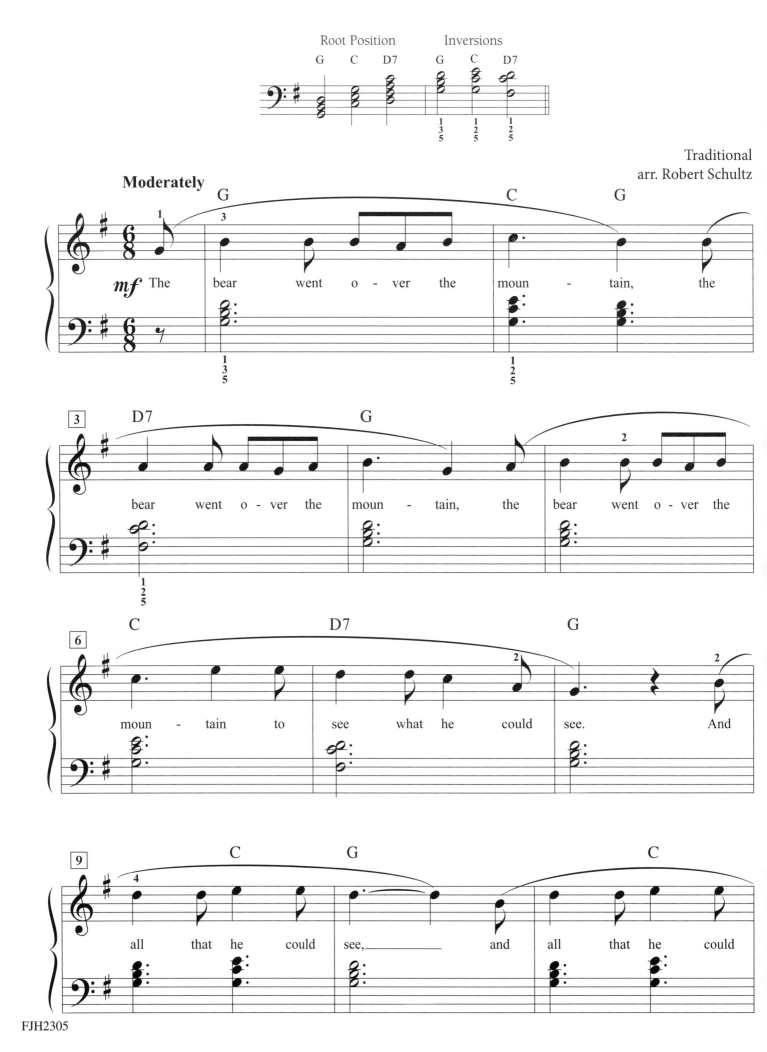

see_____ was the oth - er side of the moun - tain, the

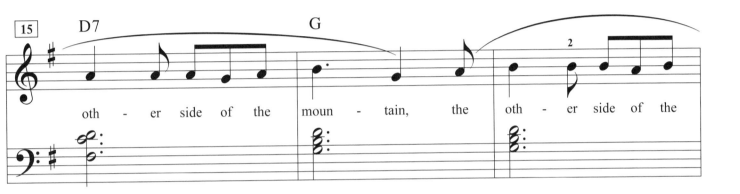

oth - er side of the moun - tain, the oth - er side of the

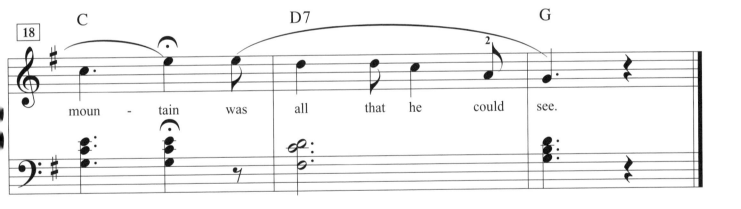

moun - tain was all that he could see.

On Top of Old Smoky

Traditional American
arr. Robert Schultz

grief,_____ but a false-heart-ed lov - er_____

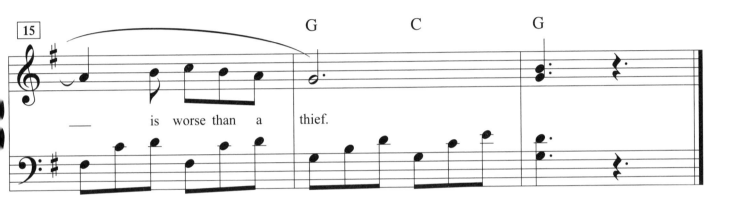

____ is worse than a thief.

When Johnny Comes Marching Home

Louis Lambert
arr. Robert Schultz